A play

Jill Woods

Samuel French—London
New York-Toronto-Hollywood

ISBN 0 573 13255 0

Please see page iv for further copyright information

CHARACTERS

Margaret. Late 40s. She is an unmarried ex-school teacher, now Mum's carer. She is rather plain, but with the potential for improvement, which she has started to realize in the form of a neat perm. Not without some spunk, she is more defeated than downtrodden.

Fay. 50-ish. Margaret's older sister. She has a shoulder-length, (dyed) blonde perm, and wears long, loose-fitting clothes. (She has rather a Seventies' look.) She is a divorcee with plenty of men in her life. She runs a wildlife sanctuary on a shoestring and is selfish and worldly-wise.

Jean. Mid-40s. The youngest sister. She is brisk, strident, middle-class, with pretentions. She takes leading roles with her local amateur dramatic society.

Mum. 75. This is a non-active, non-speaking part, as she remains asleep in bed throughout the play.

The action takes place in the upstairs bedroom of an ordinary house in West London

TIME — mid-1990s

INHERITANCE

The upstairs bedroom of an unprepossessing but neat house in West London

There is a window UC with a dressing table and stool in front of it, and a chair to either side. The bed is R, pointing into the centre of the room, with a bedside table and chair R of it. The door is L, opposite the bed, with a mirrored wardrobe L of it. There are some tea things on a tray and a framed photograph of Mum, on the bedside table, and a largish teddy bear on the bedside chair. A vase of fresh flowers is on the dressing table or windowsill

When the play begins, Mum is asleep in the bed. Margaret stands over her, patting down the sides of the bed. She then stands back and looks around

Margaret Well, Mum, that's it. That's about the best I can do. It'll never look better than this. Best duvet, fresh flowers, pine tea tray — you couldn't die in a nicer place. You'd appreciate it if you could see it. No crumbs in the carpet, no tea stains on the sheets ... Oh, and the nets are the ones you said never to use because they were too good ... Thirty years old and never seen the light of day. And you probably won't see Fay and Jean either, though if you needed something to finish you off, the shock of those two turning up'd probably do it. I s'pose you on your last legs is what they'd call a special occasion ... (*She picks up the teddy on the bedside chair and sits down wearily*) I'm tired, Mum, really tired. Plenty of times I've fancied going to sleep forever. (*She looks at Mum*) You didn't know that, did you? I've taken handfuls of pills in the last few years — just as well they were vitamin pills. Not much of an advert for them though, am I? But never mind, 'cos I'm a

"Coper", aren't I? I "cope" ... I "manage"... Oh, yes ... One of the juniors said to me once, "Miss, we think you're the cleverest teacher in the whole school," and before I could start preening, she said, "'cos you can mend fuses and unblock sinks". (*She smiles to herself*) Margaret Simkins — All Jobs Undertaken. (*She sighs*) Yes, you've had your life, whatever it was like, but what happened to mine...? (*She smooths the teddy's fur*) I spoke to Dad the other night ... Well, I s'pose it was in a dream, but it seemed very real. He said he was very sorry — for everything. He said you probably wouldn't believe him, but I was to tell you anyway. Maybe he'll be able to tell you himself before too long ... (*She sighs*) Though you won't go till you're good and ready, will you? Will of iron, that's what you've got. Maybe if I'd had one, things would have been very different ...

The doorbell rings

That'll be Fay, I suppose. (*She gets up and goes to the window*) Wonder what colour she'll be this time ... (*She looks out of the window and sniffs*) Blonde. I won't be a tick ...

Margaret exits. We hear the sounds of her descending the stairs and opening the front door

(*Off*) Hallo, Fay.

Fay (*off*) Hi. Sorry about the time. Three hours on the M4, cones all the way. Am I too late?

Margaret (*off*) Too late?

Fay (*off*) I mean, is she ... ?

Margaret (*off*) Oh, no, not yet. She's hanging on.

Fay (*off; wearily*) Oh, God.

Margaret (*off*) Sorry, but there it is. Come up.

We hear Fay and Margaret mounting the stairs

Fay (*off*) You've lost weight, Margaret.

Margaret (*off*) So would you, if you did these stairs fifty times a day.

Fay (*off*) Yes ... but not for much longer, p'raps ...

Fay and Margaret enter. Fay carries a foil-wrapped parcel

Fay hands the parcel to Margaret

A present — tofu and avocado cheesecake.

Margaret Oh.

Fay Well, you wouldn't expect me to bring chocolates, would you? I've got this new recipe book, "Volcanic Vegans" — you've never seen food like it. (*She peers at the bed and frowns*) Oh — is she awake?

Margaret (*putting the parcel on the dressing table*) Sedated. She'd started having nightmares, and then when she stopped getting me up at one o'clock in the morning for a cheese sandwich, I knew it could be critical.

Fay *A cheese sandwich?* At one o'clock in the morning?

Margaret Oh, that's relatively normal. It's been pistachio ice cream and maple syrup before now.

Fay Christ! (*She approaches the bed*) It's me, Mum — Fay. What does the doctor say?

Margaret He said for a severely arthritic seventy-five-year-old with angina who falls down the stairs and then can't wait to leave hospital, she must be made of breeze block.

Fay Oh, well, we all know that, don't we? Did she break anything?

Margaret Yes, a china mug with "World's Strongest Woman" on it. My little joke last Christmas. She'd been threatening to come down and watch *Blind Date* — (*she frowns*) — but I suppose I never really thought she meant it ...

Fay But you think she — hasn't got long?

Margaret Unless she surprises us all.

Fay (*still frowning at the bed*) Oh, I hope not ... Well, I mean, I can't get down all that often, can I ...? Did you tell her I was coming?

Margaret No. She'd never have believed it.

Fay (*swiftly*) Or cared either. (*She sighs*) I've got animals, Margaret.
You can't just leave animals. I had a concussed hedgehog
dumped on me as I was leaving home this morning. And anyway,
don't tell me her dying wish is to see me, or I'll have a heart attack
myself.

Margaret I think her dying wish is not to die, actually.

Fay (*hesitating*) And what's your wish?

Margaret Ha! I gave up throwing coins in fountains years ago. I'm
getting my rewards in heaven, so Dr Hamilton says, so that's
something to look forward to, isn't it?

Fay (*looking at Mum and sighing*) And I don't suppose she's ever
been grateful, has she?

Margaret (*sitting beside Mum*) Jean would have come last night,
but she had a rehearsal.

Fay (*groaning*) Oh, God, what is it this time — *Mary Poppins*?

Margaret *Calamity Jane*. She's playing the lead.

Fay Christ! You should have told me. I need warning of that kind
of thing.

Margaret She can only stay a couple of hours. (*She looks at Mum*)
Maybe she'll oblige and get it over with while you're both here.

Fay Well, it *would* be very convenient ... I've got two fox cubs who
need spoon-feeding every few hours, and I'd rather do it myself
... (*She leans over the bed and peers at Mum*) When you rang me,
I thought, "That's it, she's finally caved in, even *she's* not
indestructible ... " Though you never know with her ...

Margaret She's a wonderful example of a positive mental attitude,
according to Edgware General. Though I did point out that non-
stop care from a devoted daughter might have something to do
with it...

Fay (*grinning*) Devoted, eh?

Margaret Oh, I'm quite a saintly figure in the eyes of the nursing
staff. And a model of love and sacrifice, according to our
Reverend Wilkinson.

Fay 'Course you are. You're saving the NHS about four hundred
pounds a day.

Margaret Though I'm not saying it isn't nice to be *recognized* ...

Fay sits. They talk across Mum from now on

Fay (*matter-of-factly*) It had to be you, Margaret. Jean would have had her in a home before she could blink, and I would have murdered her before it even got to that.

Margaret (*quietly*) Don't you think I get angry...?

Fay And it's not as if I didn't try. I spent my whole childhood trying to please her, before I worked out it was a waste of time... (*She looks at Mum and shakes her head*) A complete waste of time...

Margaret Have you eaten?

Fay I had a granary roll at the Services. About the only thing fit for human consumption. Sometimes I think there's a mass food poisoning plot to reduce the population, masterminded by motorway service stations.

Margaret (*opening the wardrobe door*) Would you like a drink? Gin and tonic? Scotch and soda?

Fay (*laughing, looking from the bed to the wardrobe*) She doesn't ...?

Margaret (*taking out a bottle and two glasses*) We both do. Quite often.

Fay Is that how she came to fall down the stairs?

Margaret Possibly. She wasn't breathalysed at the time. (*She unscrews the bottle top*) And don't make any jokes about mother's ruin, 'cos if anyone's ruined, it's not Mother. (*She pours drinks during the following*)

Fay Ha! Fancy *her* turning to drink, of all people. You, yes, 'cos she's enough to drive anyone to the bottle...

Margaret I'm not "on the bottle". I can't afford to be, with all I have to do. We've just learnt to — appreciate the benefits, that's all.

Fay I bet.

Margaret hands Fay a drink

(*After a pause*) Does she ever talk about him?

Margaret No.

Fay Never?

Margaret Never.

Fay Arthritis can be symbolic of a rigid attitude, you know.

Margaret Well, there you are, then. (*She raises her glass*) Cheers.

Fay (*raising her glass*) What are we toasting?

Margaret I don't know. Survival?

Fay Yes, well, we all have — including her.

Margaret One of my old pupils was in the paper the other day. She'd won thousands of pounds on the lottery, and she wants a holiday in the Bahamas and a big car. No other aspirations. Why is it always people like that who get the opportunities...?

Fay Huh! Don't talk to me about money. The last time I paid a bill that didn't have a red border, I was smoking dope and had flowers in my hair. Do you know what a bale of hay costs this year? Five pounds. How do you explain to three old donkeys that you have to ration them? Not to mention vets' fees. I'm thinking of offering him my body in lieu of his last invoice.

Margaret (*going to the window and looking out*) Still, you're doing just what you always wanted to do, aren't you...?

Fay (*registering the remark*) Against all the odds.

Margaret Lots of animals ... Plenty of men ...

Fay Huh! Well, quantity doesn't mean quality as far as they're concerned, I can tell you. I've had more loyalty from the wildlife of Wiltshire. (*She looks at Margaret*) There's not much to envy in me, you know.

Margaret doesn't answer

(*Weighing her words*) I wrote to her when Martin left. I thought she'd be pleased to know that all her predictions of a disastrous marriage had come true. Gave her a chance to say, "I told you so". Quite generous, I thought, but she didn't even reply.

Margaret Well, it *was* the first letter for five years. And you did ask to borrow five hundred pounds at the same time.

Fay I was desperate. You lose all your pride when you're desperate.

Margaret (*looking away*) Yes ...

Fay And we had something in common after all — being dumped on by a bloody man. (*She pauses*) *Was* she pleased — about Martin?

Margaret She was past caring by then. She said you'd made your bed and had to lie in it. Which you have done — several times.

Fay I *wanted* a stable relationship, Margaret; I've wanted one for the last twenty years. But I'm not living like a nun while I'm waiting.

Margaret I thought Jason was your reincarnated soulmate.

Fay (*wearily*) Yes, so did I. So you'd think I'd have remembered the second time round what a complete bastard he was.

Margaret Oh, not again...

Fay He left me a note, five weeks ago. "The tide of our passion is threatening to drown us," it said, "I have to go before we both perish in the flood". Poetic, really. Then he took four slices of carrot and walnut flan to see him on his way. And to cap it all, on the same night, Bessie died of a ruptured spleen ——

Margaret gives Fay a puzzled glance. Fay sees this

— Bessie the badger. How cursed can anyone be?

Margaret (*sighing*) I expect you'll soon find a replacement ... Jason, not the badger.

Fay Yes, well there *is* Simon at the organic farm. And I do need a regular supply ...

Margaret Of what?

Fay Sex. I get headaches if I go without for too long. I've always been at the mercy of my libido.

Margaret You're disgraceful.

Fay *Disgraceful?* Look, Margaret, just because you're not ...

Margaret Not copulating every five minutes, I must be frozen solid inside? Because God gave me all the right equipment and no socket to plug into? Well, whose fault is that? Certainly not mine.

The phone rings downstairs

I'm at the mercy of Mother Nature too, you know.

Margaret exits

Fay looks defeated. She sighs

Fay (*to Mum*) What a bloody mess, eh? All of us. And who do we blame? (*She picks up the framed photo of Mum from the dressing table and speaks to it*) Well, I know who you blame, Mum — me. 'Cos if you hadn't been expecting me, you wouldn't have tied yourself to him — so I was in the frame right from the beginning. (*She sits on the stool and sighs*) But you saw it through, didn't you? And now, what have I inherited from you? A misplaced loyalty in the opposite sex. I patch 'em up, heal their emotional wounds, and then they sod off into the night. Talk about a wildlife sanctuary — more like an asylum for crippled egos. (*She looks at Mum*) Not exactly the legacy I wanted from you ... (*She goes to the wardrobe and picks up the bottle to top up her glass. She notices a rather flamboyant hat, takes it out and tries it on. She smiles at herself in the wardrobe mirror*)

Margaret returns and halts at the sight of Fay

Margaret What are you doing?

Fay This is never yours?

Margaret Well, whose else would it be?

Fay (*laughing*) It's really bold ...

Margaret I do go out sometimes, believe it or not.

Fay But it's just not you — or it never was.

Margaret Well, it is now.

Fay When do you wear it?

Margaret When I need cheering up — which is quite often.

Fay (*taking the hat off*) Church, I suppose? Are you still in the choir?

Margaret (*pouring herself another drink*) Of course I am. It's the only thing that keeps me sane.

Fay (*grinning at the hat*) All the same, I'd never have thought of you ... You've changed, Margaret.

Margaret Have I?

Fay (*returning the hat to the wardrobe*) Yes. Come to think of it, I don't remember you having a perm before ...

Margaret I'm menopausal and my hair's going thin. But at least I haven't resorted to bleach.

Fay Oh, don't get me wrong, it's a big improvement. 'Cos you've never made the best of yourself, have you? I mean, it's not as if you're unattractive ...

Margaret Thank you so much.

Fay (*sitting*) That wasn't Jean saying she can't come, by any stroke of luck, was it?

Margaret (*after a hesitation*) Er — yes. Saying she's on the way.

Fay Well, I'd better warn you, Mag, I'll do my very best to keep my mouth shut when she's here, but if she opens hers and something from *South Pacific* comes out of it, I won't be responsible for my actions.

Margaret I hardly think it's the occasion for bursting into song.

Fay She can't help herself, you know she can't. At least that's one thing you and I never inherited — a voice to wake the dead ... (*she glances at the bed*) in a manner of speaking ... (*She looks at Margaret*) I wonder who she got it from...?

The question hangs in the air

Margaret (*opening a drawer in the dressing table*) Look what I found the other day — in the tea chest, when I was rooting out Mum's net curtains ...

Margaret takes a photograph from the drawer and hands it to Fay

Fay (*quietly*) Christ ...

Margaret He looks quite respectable, doesn't he?

Fay Yes ...

Margaret Or maybe it's just the uniform ...

Fay (*gazing at the photo*) He must have been once ... respectable.

Margaret Post traumatic stress disorder, they call it today, when people turn to drink like that.

Fay Not that it would have made much difference to her, when he was laying into her.

Margaret (*quietly*) I hated him, you know. Even when he got to be a pathetic wreck. I hated his weakness and his addiction... (*Almost to herself*) And it was years before I realized that all men weren't the same ...

Fay (*after a pause in which she thinks before she speaks*) Margaret, it may not be the best time, but we must talk about money ...

Margaret (*getting up and smoothing down the duvet, as a distraction*) I wondered when that would come up.

Fay Has she ... ?

Margaret No, she hasn't made a will. She wouldn't discuss it. Every time I brought it up, she got upset and said she was going to live to a hundred anyway. So I stopped asking her.

Fay There must be quite a bit ...

Margaret Yes. A lot of it was going to her only grandson, she used to say. But then Jean had to give up bringing him here when he wouldn't stop breaking things. Artistically temperamental, I think she called it, but whatever it was, we were running out of tea cups. Then when he got through that phase and into his "destined for showbusiness" period, we hardly ever saw him. (*She looks at Mum*) She was quite bitter about that.

Fay Huh, like mother, like son. Listen, Margaret, I'm really desperate ...

Margaret (*catching a sidelong reflection of herself in the wardrobe mirror*) Do you really think I've lost weight?

Fay Eh ...?

Margaret (*looking herself up and down*) I'm a size fourteen. I bought a fitted jacket the other week — scarlet, of all things ——

Fay We've really got to ...

Margaret *And* a pair of seven denier tights — *seven* denier!

Fay (*after a hesitation, frowning*) Have you got a man?

Margaret What ...?

Fay Listen to you. Clothes, perms ——

Margaret Don't be silly.

Fay You don't have to tell me, it's none of *my* business.

Margaret (*securing some tea things on Mum's bedside tray, then picking it up*) I'd like to know when you think I have time to cultivate friendships. Why do you think I gave up work five years ago? *She's* my full time occupation.

Fay (*shrugging*) So maybe it's the milkman — *I* don't know! But you're definitely different, Margaret, in my opinion...

Margaret (*moving to the door*) Well, perhaps it's time I thought about me. Perhaps a bit of selfishness is long overdue ...

The doorbell rings

That's probably Jean.

Margaret exits

Fay (*frowning*) Jean? But she only rang five minutes ago ... (*She goes to the window and looks out*) Oh, so it is. Don't tell me she's into mobile phones now. (*To Mum*) Are you ready for this, Mum? 'Cos I'm not. I'll probably manage about an hour before I clock her one.

Jean (*off*) Margaret! Oh, my dear!

We hear Jean kiss Margaret

Margaret (*off*) Hello, Jean.

Fay pulls a face to herself

Jean (*off*) If I could have got here sooner, you know I would have. But there's so much going on! Am I ... too late?

Margaret (*off*) That's what Fay said.

Jean (*off*) She hasn't ...?

Margaret (*off*) Made a grand exit? No. I think she's waiting for a full audience.

We hear Jean and Margaret mount the stairs together

Jean (*off*) You sounded worried on the phone last night ...

Margaret (*off*) Well, I knew the shock'd set in some time ...

Margaret enters

And even she can't go on forever ...

Jean enters. She carries a handbag

Jean I wouldn't count on it... (*She sees Fay*) Fay! Darling!

Jean moves to Fay and hugs her. Fay stiffens a bit

Fay Hallo, Jean.
Jean You look so — well. How are you?
Fay Well. Thank you.
Jean And you're — er ... (*She waves a hand at Fay's hair*) Weren't you red or something, last time ...
Fay Yes. Or something.
Jean (*turning her attention to the bed*) But what about the patient? (*She moves to the bedside and frowns at Mum*) Can we say the same about the patient? Oh, no, definitely not ... Dear, oh dear ... I can see what you mean, Margaret. She's very pale ...
Margaret Though she hasn't got her rouge on. She does look a bit like a corpse without that.
Jean *Rouge?* Since when did Mother wear make-up?
Margaret Since her seventy-fifth birthday. She said she might feel it, but she was damned if she was going to look it.
Jean Oh, well — she certainly looks it now.
Fay Though she can still manage a cheese sandwich at one o'clock in the morning.
Jean It's Jean, Mum, JEAN!
Fay I've tried that. No point.
Margaret I think she's in a twilight zone. She can't respond.
Jean (*sitting by the bed and sighing*) Just like being in the womb. The beginning and end of life — just the same. (*To Margaret*) Are you all right, dear?
Margaret Me?
Jean Yes. Because if it is the end, you're the one who'll suffer the most. Are you ... prepared?
Margaret Prepared? You mean, have I got a pile of hankies washed and ironed? Assuming they'll be needed.
Jean What ...?
Margaret Because I'll be incoherent with grief? Well, you shouldn't assume that — you shouldn't.
Fay Quite right. It'll be a bigger relief to you than anyone.

Jean Well, of course you'll feel —

Margaret I won't *feel* relieved, I'll *be* relieved — of a full time nursing job for which I've never been equipped.

Jean Oh, my dear — has it been that bad?

Margaret Well, there wasn't much alternative, was there? No-one else was going to do it.

Jean Well, yes — that's true. We couldn't have had her. Derek would never have agreed.

Fay And I've seen her a dozen times in twenty-five years.

Jean So it had to be you, dear.

Margaret So everyone says.

Jean And anyway, you've been company for each other, haven't you, really?

Margaret (*drily*) Oh yes, she's been *wonderful* company.

Jean (*patronizingly*) Now *that* sounds a bit cynical to me — don't you think, Fay?

Fay (*flatly*) Surely not.

Jean And it's not surprising, Margaret, because you've been a pillar of strength, I know, and even the strongest pillar can crack in the end. So if you feel cynical, you go right ahead and be it.

Margaret Thank you.

Jean (*looking at Mum*) I know she's bad-tempered and difficult, but then, she's still Mum, isn't she...?

Margaret (*giving up on a reply*) I was going to make tea ... unless you want something from the bar.

Jean The *bar*?

Fay (*grinning and opening the wardrobe door*) Right here.

Jean Oh!

Fay Just a bit low on soda water. Mum prefers her scotch neat.

Jean Good gracious!

Margaret I'll make tea anyway.

Margaret exits with the cake

Fay (*calling after Margaret*) Lemon for me, no milk.

Jean (*shaking her head*) So it's come to that, has it?

Fay Oh, I don't think she's sozzled *every* night.

Jean And Margaret as well. How awful.

Fay (*topping her glass up*) Don't tell me you never reach for the bottle in times of crisis, Jean.

Jean I most certainly do not. And I've had plenty of reason to in the last few months, don't think I haven't. Ha! I'd be an alcoholic by that reckoning. But Derek and I have come through everything without *that* sort of help.

Fay (*after a hesitation*) You ... and Derek?

Jean No, no, not Derek and I like *that* — Derek and I as a team! We've faced everything that's happened together, positively, that's what I mean.

Fay Oh. Good. (*She sits near the window*)

Jean I know you and Margaret think I lead a charmed life, but you haven't been at the mercy of the free market like we have. We never thought a senior consultant with thirty years in property development would ever be made redundant, but we were wrong.

Fay (*raising an eyebrow*) Derek ...?

Jean Rationalization, or streamlining, is what they call it. And when they say how much they appreciate all you've done for the company's success, you want to spit in their eye. Oh, not that Derek did — he was very dignified about the whole thing — but he felt like it, I can tell you. And then, of course, everyone thinks he's walked away with a fortune, but he hasn't, not when you think he'd only been there ten years and he might never be employed again. (*She draws a long breath*) Anyway, as I said, once he'd got over the shock, we faced it positively, and now he's decided just where his future lies — in crime.

Fay *Crime?*

Jean Burglar alarms, security systems. It's a growth industry with guaranteed expansion, whatever the economic climate.

Fay Oh. I thought you meant ... Derek and a balaclava.

Jean And as it happens, he *has* got his eye on a franchise ... if we can just raise the collateral. So I did wonder, in the circumstances, whether there might be a bit of help — you know — round the corner ... (*She slowly looks round at Mum*)

Fay So did I. Wonder. I'm every bit as desperate as you are, Jean.

Jean (*half-mouthing the words*) I suppose she must have ——

Fay No. There's no will. Though I believe her only grandson might have done quite well if he hadn't been a bit of a disappointment to Grandma.

Jean If you mean Adrian, *I* hardly ever see him, never mind her. He's choreographing in Dubai right now. He's in constant demand. (*Slowly*) So it would be the three of us who would ... without any complications...

Fay (*looking round at Mum*) And sooner rather than later, maybe ...

Jean (*almost to herself*) I'd hate to have to get rid of that Sierra ...

Fay By the way, did you telephone ten minutes ago, from a mobile?

Fay Me? No.

Fay Mmm, that's what I thought. Margaret took a phone call and said it was you. But I had a feeling it wasn't ...

Fay (*frowning*) What do you mean?

Fay I don't know — or at least, I might have an idea. Don't you think she's different?

Jean Different?

Fay She's had her hair done and lost weight, and she's wearing big hats. What does that usually mean?

Jean (*laughing as she realizes*) *Margaret?* Never!

Fay She never actually denied it when I asked her — but why would she want to keep it a secret? Something's going on.

Jean (*laughing*) Well, it wouldn't be *that*! Really, dear, I can't imagine anything less likely ...

Margaret enters with a tray of tea things, including plates and forks and the unwrapped cake

Margaret Less likely than what?

Jean and Fay exchange startled glances

Jean Er ... er ... than Mum pulling through ... the way she looks ...

Margaret (*settling the tea tray down on the dressing table*) Well, that's what we're all hoping for, I suppose, isn't it? That she won't, I mean.

Jean What ...?

Margaret No point in pretending. Fay's got fox cubs to feed, you're in the middle of rehearsals, and I'm worn out. So it'd be handy if she didn't hang about.

Jean Oh. Well ...

Margaret If there's one thing *I've* inherited from her in the last few years, it's the art of plain speaking. And the avoidance of hypocrisy. Who's for tofu cheesecake?

Fay Oh, Margaret, I brought that for you.

Margaret Oh, *I'll* never eat it — all. We can make a start on it ... (*She slices the cheesecake during the following and puts the slices on plates*)

Jean (*getting up to peer at it*) *What* cheesecake ... ?

Fay Tofu and avocado.

Jean (*frowning*) Oh. Doesn't look like cheesecake ...

Margaret I'm sure Fay will take full responsibility for any after effects, won't you, dear?

Fay (*raising her eyes*) What do you think — that I'm going to poison you for your inheritance?

Margaret Just a shame that Mum's missing out, with her tastebuds.

Margaret hands a plate of cake to Jean

Jean (*looking at the cake uncertainly*) Ye ... es ...

Margaret She could do with a change from Mars Bar sandwiches ...

Margaret hands a plate of cake to Fay

Fay (*groaning*) Oh, my God...

Margaret Tuck in. (*Without enthusiasm*) There's loads here ...

Fay forks up the cheesecake with ease, while Jean and Margaret do so hesitantly. They react slowly and obviously; they both dislike it

Jean Well, I'm sorry, Fay, but I'm afraid I'll have to join Margaret in not being a hypocrite. It's ... Well ...

Margaret Indescribable. (*She pours cups of tea during the following*)

Jean And I'm very adventurous about food. Derek and I have tried every type of cuisine — but — well ...

Fay Just as well I didn't bring the seaweed pâté, then.

Jean I suppose it's symbolic of our different lifestyles really, isn't it? You in your hippy heaven, and me and Margaret in suburbia. So you mustn't be offended, dear.

Fay Perish the thought.

Margaret puts a teaspoon of sugar into Jean's cup of tea

Jean (*to Margaret*) Put an extra spoon in, to take away the ... (*She gives a tight little smile to Fay*)

Margaret Just as well both of you aren't staying for a meal. I'm out of caviar and lentils.

Jean (*brightening*) And have you told Fay *why* I can't stay? Have you told her about my *big* commitment ...?

Margaret Er ...

Jean My starring role ...?

Margaret hands Fay a cup of tea. Fay gives Margaret a desperate grimace

Margaret Yes ... yes. I told her.

Jean Opening Thursday night — all seats sold! If you wanted a ticket you couldn't get one! Oh, my dears, it'll be the biggest night of my life! Even my Dolly Levi in 1989 can't compare. 'Cos I've always wanted Calamity — she was made for me.

Fay (*getting up and putting down her teacup*) I must go to the bog.

Margaret hands Jean a cup of tea

Jean (*ploughing on*) Janine, our producer, said there was really no competition for the part. I'm a natural Calamity.

Fay heads for the exit

Fay (*to herself*) And how.

Fay exits

Jean I'm actually ten years older than our Wild Bill Hickock, but you'd never believe it — no one can.

Margaret Ugh! All that make-up. (*She sits on the stool and stirs her tea*)

Jean (*frowning*) No, dear, I mean *without* make-up. My whole *persona* is right, that's what I'm saying. And you can't tackle *My Secret Love* if your top register isn't working. Oh, I wish you could have come — and Mum. She's only ever seen me in the chorus of a G and S.

Margaret She doesn't like musicals. She says you're just getting into the plot when someone bursts into song and ruins it. She wouldn't have come.

Jean What with Adrian being away ... And Derek never comes, of course. He can't stand the tension, in case something awful happens.

Margaret Like what?

Jean Well, anything. The scenery collapsing, or someone forgetting their lines. His blood pressure rockets, being on the edge of his seat all the time. (*She looks at Mum*) Of course, if something happens here ... I mean, if she should ... Before Thursday...

Margaret The show must go on.

Jean Exactly. After all, I am the star. (*She puts down her cup and stands up*) Speaking of which, I had planned a little surprise for Mum, if she'd been sitting up and taking notice ... But it needn't go to waste ... (*She pulls a toy gun out of her handbag*)

Margaret Oh, my God!

Jean slides the gun into a pocket of her skirt, as if into a holster, and stands with her legs apart

Jean (*adopting an American accent*) How'dya like a li'le ol' rendition of the opening number, huh?

Margaret What ...?

Jean Right here and free of charge! Whaddaya say?

Margaret Er ...

Jean Ah cain always do with a li'le practice mahself! Come on now, let's clear the stage ...

Jean moves the chairs back to make a wide space. Margaret moves and sits on one of the chairs by the dressing table

   Fay enters

Jean (*gaily*) Come and take a front row seat, dear, show's just starting.

Fay What ...?

Margaret We're going to be entertained.

Fay (*groaning quietly*) Oh, my God ...

Jean (*in an American accent*) Could be just what the doctor ordered!

Fay He'd be struck off.

Jean Ever the cynic, dear. Just as well I'm immune.

Fay sits to the other side of the dressing table from Margaret

   That's it, just there ... and, er ... (*She picks up the teddy and plonks it in between the other two, on the stool*) There we are, a full house!

Margaret What about — accompaniment?

Fay (*swiftly*) *I'm* not joining in.

Jean I'm a trained singer, Margaret, I don't *need* accompaniment. Now, just use your imagination ... (*American*) The scene is The Golden Garter, Deadwood City, Dakota Territory — and Calamity's in town!

Jean sings "The Deadwood Stage" with plenty of accompanying action. Margaret tries to look interested. Fay can't quite believe it

Jean finishes with a flourish and a bow. There is a moment's silence, before Margaret claps hesitantly, though Fay doesn't

Margaret (*without much enthusiasm*) Bravo.

Jean Thank you. Thank you.

Fay (*staring*) Unbelievable.

Jean Will I do?

Margaret Yes — oh, yes.

Jean When I've got the fringed jacket and boots on, I'm her! Janine says it's Doris Day to the life! And I'll have lost a stone by the last performance, you know, through sheer nervous tension.

Margaret Well, you've certainly got a ... got to *have* a nerve, yes.

Jean She says I really should have gone into showbusiness. It's been a terrible waste of potential.

Margaret (*getting up*) And what did Mum think? What does she say ... ?

Fay Speechless, I should think.

Margaret (*leaning over the bed*) Mmmm, I'm afraid so ...

Jean I expect it's penetrated at some level, it's bound to.

Margaret Yes, well, maybe she'll die happy now. Prophetic, perhaps, *The Deadwood Stage*.

Fay What a way to go ... er, on a high note, I mean.

Margaret Thank you, dear, anyway. I'm sure Fay and I would have come if we could, wouldn't we, Fay?

Fay (*aghast*) Eh...? Oh, well, *I* couldn't, but you could go, Margaret. It's not that far for you. Get next door to look after Mum if she's still ——

Margaret I hardly think so.

Jean Oh, of course you could, dear, whyever not?

Fay (*cautiously*) It's not as if you'd have to go alone, is it ...? You'd have someone to go with, wouldn't you ...?

Margaret (*putting the tea things on to the tray*) It's out of the question.

Fay Wouldn't you ...?

There is a marked silence. Margaret avoids the eyes of the others and concentrates on the tea tray

Jean (*slowly*) *Would* you, dear...?

Margaret (*rounding on the others*) No! No, I wouldn't! I wouldn't have someone to go with, all right?

Fay and Jean stare at Margaret

I'd have to go on my own — like I've always had to —
always. (*Her voice breaks, she puts a hand to her mouth and
her head drops*)

There is a stunned silence

I haven't got a man — that's what you're asking, isn't it? I
wish I had, but I haven't!

Jean Oh, dear ...

Fay We just thought you ——

Margaret Having your hair done and wearing fancy hats doesn't
mean you've got a man. It just means you want to look nice for
someone who you wish ... You wish ... But you know he never
will, because you've got "spinster of this parish" written all over
you; full time nurse, a model of love and sacrifice ... (*Her voice
breaks on a sob, and she starts crying*)

Jean and Fay stare at Margaret wordlessly

And it's even worse when you know — you know you might
have stood a chance, because he likes you and he's on his own
too ... (*She blows her nose*)

Fay Oh, Margaret...

Jean (*patronizingly*) Oh, *dear*!

Margaret But there's no point in hoping ... No point...

Jean Is it — someone we know...?

Margaret (*rounding on Jean*) How can it be someone you know?
I've never had anyone, have I? No-one ever came here, until ...

The words hang in the air

Fay (*hesitantly*) Until what ...?

Margaret Until Mum got worse and — couldn't go to church.

Fay and Jean look at each other

Fay And ...?

Margaret And he started calling round — for tea. And saying he understood if I couldn't make choir rehearsals ...

Fay (*frowning*) You mean ...

Margaret I'm such an unselfish person, he says, but I'm not! I'm not unselfish at all! Because I know if it wasn't for her we might ... And sometimes I hate her for it.

Fay (*slowly*) The Vicar...?

Margaret And yet it's because of her that he comes here at all, so maybe I should be grateful ...

Jean Oh, my *dear*...

Fay Oh, Christ!

Margaret And *He's* not been much help, either!

Fay Was that the phone call...?

Margaret (*nodding and sniffing*) He's very caring — always asking after her ...

Fay I'm so sorry, Margaret.

Jean Yes, dear, of course we are. We should never have just assumed you were happy without ... Well ...

Fay Sex.

Jean A *man* — company. I mean, *I've* always thought you were naturally ... Well ...

Fay Celibate.

Jean Thank you, dear. I think Margaret knows what I mean.

Fay Of course she does. You mean, we both should have realized she wasn't happy with her virgin lot ... my God, *I* should have, of all people. Not that there was much we could have done, Margaret, but at least we should have been *aware* ...

Margaret (*blowing her nose*) There's nothing anyone can do. It's my problem. First him, then her — they've both been my problem.

Fay (*realizing; slowly*) But what if she — dies? If you were free — ? Wouldn't that make a difference ...?

Jean (*helpfully*) Yes. No millstone?

Margaret (*quietly*) Yes.

Fay Yes. (*Slowly*) Margaret, how *did* she come to fall down the stairs ...?

Margaret (*vaguely*) What...?
Jean (*realizing*) Fay!
Fay How ...?
Jean It was an accident!
Fay Was it? Was it an accident, Margaret?
Margaret Probably.
Fay (*frowning*) What do you mean, probably?
Margaret I left something on the stairs — a book. (*Almost to herself*) I must have forgotten to move it when she said she was coming down ... I must have done ...

Her words hang in the air. Jean throws a hand to her mouth, speechless

I can't be expected to think of everything, can I?
Fay (*slowly*) No. 'Course you can't. Maybe *we'd* have been just as... forgetful, in your position. (*She looks at Mum*) If we couldn't see a way out ... (*She looks squarely back at the others*) And we're *all* in need of our inheritance, aren't we ...?

Jean is speechless. Margaret looks at the floor. There is a marked silence

Suddenly, Mum stirs in the bed and seems to speak. They all turn to look at her

Jean Mum...? (*She goes to the side of the bed*) Mum...? (*She bends over Mum*)

Mum says something inaudible

What is it...? (*She bends closer to Mum, then straightens slowly and stares wide-eyed at the other two*) She said ... She said, could she have a cheese sandwich ...?

Black-out

FURNITURE AND PROPERTY LIST

On stage: Dressing table. *On it*: vase of fresh flowers. *In drawer*: photograph
Stool
Three chairs. *On bedside chair*: largish teddy bear
Bed
Bedside table. *On it*: tea things on tray, framed photograph of Mum
Mirrored wardrobe. *In it*: bottles of gin and whisky, glasses, flamboyant hat

Off stage: Foil-wrapped parcel containing cheesecake (**Fay**)
Plates and forks to add to tray of tea things (**Margaret**)

Personal: **Jean**: handbag containing toy gun

LIGHTING PLOT

Practicals required: nil
One interior with window backing. The same throughout

To open: General interior lighting with light on window backing

No cues

EFFECTS PLOT

Cue 1   **Margaret**: " ... would have been very different ..."   (Page 2)
               Doorbell

Cue 2   **Margaret**: "Certainly not mine."   (Page 7)
               Phone rings

Cue 3   **Margaret**: " ... selfishness is long overdue."   (Page 11)
               Doorbell